THE ULTIMATE
CHELSEA FC
TRIVIA BOOK

A Collection of Amazing Trivia Quizzes
and Fun Facts for Die-Hard Blues Fans!

Ray Walker

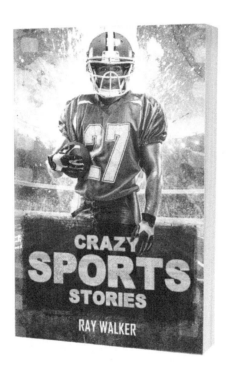

CONTENTS

INTRODUCTION

Chelsea FC is one of the most celebrated and famous football clubs in the UK and across the world and has been thrilling fans at Stamford Bridge since being formed back in 1905. The team has been one of the most consistent on the globe in the past 20 years, with numerous league titles to its name as well as several domestic and European cup triumphs.

Typically known as "the Pensioners" in the early days and now generally referred to as "the Blues," this top-flight London-based side possesses a long and legendary history.

Many of the world's top players have suited up for Chelsea over the past century, and the outfit has employed a long list of first-rate managers. Who can ever forget the likes of such charismatic figures as Willie Foulke, Roy Bentley, Peter Bonetti, Charlie Cooke, Peter Osgood, Frank Lampard, Michael Essien, John Obi Mikel, Didier Drogba, Ashley Cole, Petr Čech, Michael Ballack, Ray Wilkins, Jimmy Greaves, Ron Harris, Danny Blanchflower, Glenn Hoddle, and José Mourinho?

Chelsea fans did have to endure plenty of lean trophy-less periods early on, as it took about 50 years to win the first top-flight league title and then another 50 before they repeated the achievement. But, once the drought was snapped, the team continued to steadily add more silverware to the trophy room.

This includes being crowned champions of Europe in dramatic fashion in 2011-12 when beating Bayern Munich of Germany right in their own backyard.

There's no doubt Chelsea supporters are second to none when it comes to displaying passion and fierce loyalty to the team. They have supported the club through thick and thin for well over 100 years now and will surely continue to do so for the next 100.

This Chelsea FC trivia and fact book contains an abundance of information covering the club's history from its humble beginnings up to February 2021, during the days of the Covid-19 pandemic.

The book offers 12 unique chapters with each of them featuring a separate quiz. Each chapter will challenge fans on Chelsea history with a combination of 20 multiple-choice and true-false brain teasers with the correct answers being revealed on a later page.

Every quiz chapter also provides 10 lighthearted historical "Did You Know?" facts about the club's history, players, managers, transfers, records, trophy wins, and more.

Blues supporters can quickly sharpen up their quiz-taking skills by reading the book to relive the famous moments and refresh their memories. Hopefully, you'll even be able to learn something new with each page you turn.

These quizzes and facts are the perfect way to prepare yourself for Chelsea quiz and trivia challenges from family members, friends, and fellow fans.

We hope you'll enjoy this historic journey through the ages to help you realize why you've always been such a passionate, loyal supporter of the amazing Chelsea FC.

CHAPTER 1:

ORIGINS & HISTORY

QUIZ TIME!

1. In what year was Chelsea FC founded?

    a. 1908

    b. 1905

    c. 1900

    d. 1897

2. Chelsea originally played in the Southern League for the club's first four years of existence.

    a. True

    b. False

3. Who was the key founder of Chelsea?

    a. Richard McCabe

    b. Joseph Mears

    c. Henry Norris

    d. Henry Augustus Mears

4. Who scored the first league goal in the club's history?

a. James Watson

b. Martin Moran

c. John Tait Robertson

d. Jimmy Windridge

5. What was the original color of the team's kit?

a. Navy blue

b. Yellow

c. White and red

d. Eton blue

6. Against which club did Chelsea play its first league match?

a. Stockport County FC

b. Blackpool

c. Lincoln City FC

d. Manchester United

7. After a deal to rent Stamford Bridge Athletics Ground to local club Fulham fell through, the owners formed Chelsea FC to play at the stadium instead.

a. True

b. False

8. How many times has the club made a significant change to its crest?

a. 2

b. 4

c. 6

d. 7

9. What was the outcome of the side's first league match?

    a. 5-1 win
    b. draw
    c. loss
    d. 2-0 win

10. Chelsea's first official win came during a friendly match against which side?

    a. Bradford City FC
    b. Liverpool FC
    c. Sheffield United
    d. Blackburn Rovers

11. Which was NOT one of the names that management considered before settling on Chelsea FC?

    a. Kensington FC
    b. London FC
    c. Stamford Bridge FC
    d. North Fulham Athletics

12. The club earned the nickname "the Pensioners" for featuring an army veteran on their first crest design.

    a. True
    b. False

13. Chelsea played which squad in its first Premier League match?

    a. Oldham Athletic
    b. Arsenal
    c. Norwich City
    d. Ipswich Town

14. Which player scored Chelsea's first goal in the Premier League?

   a. Michael Harford
   b. John Spencer
   c. Nigel Spackman
   d. Andy Myers

15. What was the outcome of Chelsea's first Premier League encounter?

   a. 2-2 draw
   b. 3-0 loss
   c. 2-0 win
   d. draw

16. Chelsea has played at Stamford Bridge stadium since the club was founded.

   a. True
   b. False

17. How many times has the team been relegated as of 2020?

   a. 3
   b. 4
   c. 6
   d. 10

18. In which season was Chelsea relegated to the Second Division for the first time?

   a. 1947-48
   b. 1923-24
   c. 1909-10
   d. 1907-08

19. How many matches did the squad win in its first-ever league season?

    a. 10

    b. 15

    c. 19

    d. 23

20. Chelsea was NOT one of the 22 teams to join the Premier League in 1992-93.

    a. True

    b. False

QUIZ ANSWERS

1. B – 1905

2. B – False

3. D – Henry Augustus Mears

4. C – John Tait Robertson

5. D – Eton blue

6. A – Stockport County FC

7. A – True

8. B – 4

9. C – 1-0 loss

10. B – Liverpool FC

11. D – North Fulham Athletics

12. A – True

13. A – Oldham Athletic

14. A – Michael Harford

15. D – 1-1 draw

16. A – True

17. C – 6

18. C – 1909-10

19. D – 23

20. B – False

DID YOU KNOW?

1. The Chelsea Football Club of the English Premier League was formed on March 10, 1905, in an upstairs room at the Rising Sun Pub on Fulham Road in London, England. The team's nicknames are "the Blues" and "the Pensioners." Chelsea FC is currently owned by Russian-Israeli businessman and politician Roman Abramovich.

2. Among the founding directors of Chelsea were millionaire owner Henry Augustus "Gus" Mears, along with his brother Joseph, their brother-in-law Henry Boyer, Alfred Janes, Frederick Parker, and Mears's nephew Edwin, who operated the Rising Sun Pub.

3. Gus Mears bought the Stamford Bridge athletics stadium in 1904, hoping to transform it into a soccer venue. He intended to rent the ground out to Fulham FC, but after a deal he had in place fell through, Mears decided to simply form a new club. This is how Chelsea FC originally came to be with the name coming from a nearby London borough.

4. When deciding on the team's name, Mears and his crew considered Kensington FC, London FC, and Stamford Bridge FC before settling on Chelsea. The club was soon elected to the English Football League and played its first official match away to Stockport on September 25, 1905, which resulted in a 1-0 loss. The Division 2 contest

attracted 7,000 fans, which was then a club record for Stockport.

5. Stamford Bridge, which sits on Fulham Road, was created for athletic competitions in 1877. Famous architect Archibald Leitch then designed it into a soccer stadium, and it's been home to Chelsea since 1905. The Blues opened the ground with a 4-0 victory over Liverpool in a friendly match in September 1905 and attracted 67,000 fans to a game against Manchester United on Good Friday 1906.

6. Chelsea earned promotion to the Football League's First Division at the conclusion of the 1906-07 season, its second in the league, when the club finished runner-up in Division 2. During the club's first few seasons, the players wore shirts of Eton blue, the horse racing colors of club president Lord Cadogan. The team's current home kit colors are royal blue shirts and shorts with white socks.

7. The Blues reached the FA Cup final for the first time in 1915 but lost to Sheffield United at Manchester United's Old Trafford ground. The first major trophy didn't arrive until 40 years later when the squad won the First Division title in 1954-55. It would be another 50 years before the side won the top-flight league again, in 2004-05.

8. Chelsea quickly became a popular club and one of the best supported in London and the nation. In the late 1910s, the team was attracting over 40,000 fans per game on average. This made Chelsea the first team in Britain to

average that many supporters to its matches. The side's first piece of silverware was hoisted in 1915-16 when it captured the London Combination. This was a regional league that operated while first-class competition was halted during World War I.

9. The first taste of success for the club in Europe came in 1970-71 when the Blues captured the European Cup Winners' Cup with a 2-1 win over Real Madrid in Piraeus, Greece, on May 21, 1971. The two teams had played two days earlier at the same venue, but a replay was needed after the contest ended in a 1-1 draw after extra time.

10. Chelsea also has a women's team, which was originally named the Chelsea Ladies Football Club when it was established in 1992. The squad has been affiliated with Chelsea FC since 2004, with the first team competing in the FA Women's Super League and the reserve side playing in the FA WSL Development League Southern Division. The Chelsea FC Women's side plays its home matches at Kingsmeadow in Kingston upon Thames.

CHAPTER 2:

THE CAPTAIN CLASS

QUIZ TIME!

1. Who succeeded Gary Cahill as captain in 2019?

    a. Andreas Christensen

    b. Kurt Zouma

    c. César Azpilicueta

    d. Willian

2. Chelsea has had 69 full-time captains as of 2020.

    a. True

    b. False

3. Who captained Chelsea to its first-ever top-flight league title?

    a. Roy Bentley

    b. Ken Armstrong

    c. Derek Saunders

    d. John McNichol

4. After leaving Chelsea, Andy Townsend went on to captain which club?

   a. Middlesbrough FC
   b. Aston Villa
   c. West Bromwich Albion
   d. Southampton FC

5. How many team trophies did Dennis Wise win with the club?

   a. 3
   b. 5
   c. 2
   d. 6

6. Who captained Chelsea to five Premier League titles?

   a. Ron Harris
   b. Dennis Wise
   c. Roy Bentley
   d. John Terry

7. Marcel Desailly captained AC Milan before being appointed skipper of Chelsea.

   a. True
   b. False

8. Which player was vice-captain in 2014-15?

   a. Diego Costa
   b. Willian
   c. Didier Drogba
   d. Cesc Fàbregas

9. Who captained Chelsea to the club's 1988-89 Division 2 title?

   a. Frank Blunstone
   b. Peter Nicholas
   c. Graham Roberts
   d. Colin Pates

10. Which former captain currently owns the Chelsea record for most games played?

   a. John Terry
   b. Frank Blunstone
   c. Micky Droy
   d. Ron Harris

11. As of February 2021, how many full-time captains has the team appointed since 2019?

   a. 0
   b. 1
   c. 2
   d. 3

12. Gary Cahill replaced John Terry as captain in 2017.

   a. True
   b. False

13. Which player captained Chelsea in their first Premier League season?

   a. Dennis Wise
   b. Andy Townsend
   c. Peter Nicholas
   d. Marcel Desailly

14. Whom did Ron Harris replace as captain?

    a. Terry Venables
    b. Micky Droy
    c. Ken Armstrong
    d. Frank Upton

15. Which skipper recorded two songs that reached the top 50 in the UK singles chart?

    a. Graham Roberts
    b. Terry Venables
    c. Roy Bentley
    d. William Foulke

16. Gary Cahill won four team trophies as captain of Chelsea.

    a. True
    b. False

17. Who was John Terry's vice-captain in the 2009-10 campaign?

    a. Frank Lampard
    b. Joe Cole
    c. Nemanja Matić
    d. Ashley Cole

18. Which player was temporarily appointed captain after John Terry was handed a four-match ban in 2012?

    a. Ryan Bertrand
    b. Florent Malouda
    c. Paulo Ferreira
    d. Petr Čech

19. What was Ron Harris's nickname?

    a. Hurricane
    b. Chopper
    c. Rowdy Ron
    d. Hatchet

20. Marcel Desailly was born in Ghana but played nationally for France.

    a. True
    b. False

QUIZ ANSWERS

1. C – César Azpilicueta

2. B – False

3. A – Roy Bentley

4. B – Aston Villa

5. D – 6

6. D – John Terry

7. B – False

8. C – Didier Drogba

9. C – Graham Roberts

10. D – Ron Harris

11. B – 1

12. A – True

13. A – Dennis Wise

14. A – Terry Venables

15. B – Terry Venables

16. B – False

17. A – Frank Lampard

18. D – Petr Čech

19. B – Chopper

20. A – True

DID YOU KNOW?

1. It's believed that just under 120 players have worn the captain's armband for Chelsea from the time the club joined the Football League in 1905 to February 2021. Some of these players were considered full-time skippers, while others may have served as acting captain for just a handful of games or so. Goalkeeper William Foulke reportedly wore the armband in the club's first season, and other goalies who have captained the team at one time or another include Peter Bonetti, Dave Beasant, Carlo Cudicini, and Petr Čech.

2. English international defender John Terry was the club's most successful captain, as he led the side to five Premier League titles, four FA Cups, three League Cups, one UEFA Europa League, and one European Champions League. He played 717 games between 1998 and 2017, and, with 67 goals, he's also the team's all-time highest-scoring defender. He was appointed skipper when Marcel Desailly departed in 2004-05, and he was named Player of the Year by his fellow professionals that season. Terry won the UEFA Best Defender of the Year award three times and was named to the FIFPro World XI five times. He also captained England and Aston Villa, where he finished his career.

3. After joining the Blues from Wimbledon in 1990 for £1.6 million, central midfielder Dennis Wise became captain in

1993 and played 445 times with the side. The English international scored 76 goals and displayed excellent leadership abilities, even though he was known for his fiery temper. Wise led his teammates to six trophies: two FA Cups, a League Cup, the UEFA Cup Winners' Cup, the UEFA Super Cup, and an FA Charity Shield. The bundle of energy was sold to Leicester City in 2001 when new manager Claudio Ranieri wanted a younger squad.

4. Defender/midfielder Marcel Desailly was born in Ghana but played nationally for France. He joined Chelsea in 1998 from AC Milan for £4.6 million and spent the next six seasons at Stamford Bridge, chipping in with seven goals in 222 appearances. He skippered the squad between 2001 and 2004 and was known as "the Rock" due to his solid defensive play. Desailly was a tough tackler who helped the team win the European Super Cup in 1998, the FA Cup in 1999-2000, and the FA Charity Shield in 2000. He left London in 2004 to play in Qatar with Al-Gharafa, where he was appointed club captain.

5. Defender Ron Harris played the most games in Chelsea history as of 2021 with 795 of them between 1962 and 1980 after helping the club win the FA Youth Cup in 1961. He also helped the first team win six trophies, including the European Cup Winners' Cup and two FA and League Cups. The 5-foot-8-inch Harris had one of the greatest nicknames in the sport; he was known as "Chopper" because of his no-nonsense, tough-tackling ways. He has also played the most league games with the club at 657

and had the most FA Cup appearances with 64. Harris left in 1980 to join Brentford as player-coach and later became a professional greyhound trainer.

6. Midfielder Terry Venables won the FA Youth Cup in 1960 and 1961 and then played with the senior side as a teenager until leaving for Tottenham Hotspur in 1966. The skipper won the League Cup in 1964-65 and helped the team earn promotion to the top flight in 1962-63 after being relegated a year earlier. After retiring as a player, he went on to manage several teams. Venables was vice-chairman of the Professional Footballers' Association in the 1970s, co-authored five novels, co-created the ITV detective series *Hazell*, worked as a television pundit, recorded a World Cup single with the band Rider in 2002 called "England Crazy," which reached number 46 in the UK charts and also reached number 23 in the charts in 2010 after recording "If I Can Dream."

7. Jack Harrow was the first player to appear in 300 games with Chelsea after joining in March 1911 for £50 from Croydon Common. The forward-turned-defender captained the side for much of his playing career until it ended in 1926 and was known for his speed and free kicks. He played 334 games with the side, scoring a handful of goals, and led the team to its first FA Cup final in 1915. After hanging up his boots, Harrow joined the club's training staff until 1938.

8. Graham Roberts played with Chelsea from 1988 to 1990 after arriving from the Glasgow Rangers and was made

team captain. The defender cost £475,000, and it was money well spent, as he helped the side capture the Second Division championship in 1988-89. Roberts had a knack for scoring goals: He tallied 23 times in his 83 appearances for the Blues. He left Stamford Bridge for West Bromwich Albion and later became a football manager with stints on Pakistan's and Nepal's national squads.

9. After graduating from the youth system, defender/ midfielder John Hollins played 592 games with Chelsea in two separate stints. He made his pro debut as a 17-year- old in 1963 and remained until 1975, helping the side win a League Cup, FA Cup, and European Cup Winners' Cup. Hollins was a supreme playmaker who chipped in with 64 goals of his own. Hollins, who always led by example, was voted Chelsea's Player of the Year in 1970 and 1971 and left for the Queens Park Rangers in 1975. He returned in 1983-84 and helped the team win the Second Division before retiring. Hollins became a Chelsea coach and then manager of the club until March 1988.

10. Spanish international César Azpilicueta took over the full- time captaincy in 2019 when fellow defender Gary Cahill departed. He joined in the summer of 2012 and helped the team win the Europa League in his first season. He also helped win the Premier League and League Cup double in 2014-15 and the Premier League and FA Cup double in 2016-17. Azpilicueta wasn't finished there, as he skippered the squad to another Europa League crown in

2018-19. As of February 2021, he had played over 400 games with the Blues and was the Players' Player of the Year in 2013-14 and a member of the 2018-19 Europa League Squad of the Season.

CHAPTER 3:

AMAZING MANAGERS

QUIZ TIME!

1. Who was Chelsea's first manager?

    a. David Calderhead

    b. Leslie Knighton

    c. John Tait Robertson

    d. William Lewis

2. Sir Alex Ferguson once managed the side to an FA Cup title.

    a. True

    b. False

3. Which manager led the club to its first league title?

    a. Leslie Knighton

    b. Billy Birrell

    c. Ted Drake

    d. Tommy Docherty

4. Carlo Ancelotti managed which Italian side before being hired by the Blues?

   a. AC Milan

   b. S.S. Lazio

   c. Parma Calcio

   d. S.S.C. Napoli

5. Who was appointed interim manager in 2012?

   a. Guus Hiddink

   b. Rafael Benítez

   c. Ray Wilkins

   d. Steve Holland

6. Who was the club's first manager to hail from outside of the British Isles?

   a. Luiz Felipe Scolari

   b. Avram Grant

   c. José Mourinho

   d. Ruud Gullit

7. Chelsea has had four player-managers as of 2020.

   a. True

   b. False

8. How many trophies did Gianluca Vialli win with the team?

   a. 1

   b. 3

   c. 5

   d. 7

9. Whose stint as Chelsea manager was shorter?

    a. David Webb
    b. André Villas-Boas
    c. Guus Hiddink
    d. Danny Blanchflower

10. Antonio Conte went on to manage which club following his departure from Chelsea?

    a. Inter Milan
    b. S.S. Arezzo
    c. Atalanta
    d. Liverpool FC

11. In terms of silverware won, who has been Chelsea's most successful manager as of 2021?

    a. Gianluca Vialli
    b. José Mourinho
    c. Roberto Di Matteo
    d. Carlo Ancelotti

12. Roberto Di Matteo became Aston Villa's manager after being fired by Chelsea.

    a. True
    b. False

13. Who replaced Maurizio Sarri as the boss in July 2019?

    a. Thomas Tuchel
    b. Ron Stuart
    c. Dave Sexton
    d. Frank Lampard

14. Which club was Claudio Ranieri manager of before joining the Blues in 2000?

    a. ACF Fiorentina
    b. Fulham FC
    c. Atlético Madrid
    d. Valencia CF

15. As of 2020, how many Chelsea managers have won a major league or UEFA trophy with the club?

    a. 8
    b. 22
    c. 7
    d. 14

16. David Calderhead has been Chelsea's longest-serving manager as of 2020.

    a. True
    b. False

17. How many total team trophies did José Mourinho win with the side?

    a. 13
    b. 12
    c. 8
    d. 5

18. Who was appointed manager in 2011 after Carlo Ancelotti and Chelsea parted ways?

    a. José Mourinho
    b. Roberto Di Matteo

c. André Villas-Boas

d. Guus Hiddink

19. How many full-time Chelsea managers hailed from Italy?

   a. 1

   b. 6

   c. 8

   d. 15

20. Glenn Hoddle left his job as Chelsea manager in 1996 to manage the English men's national team.

   a. True

   b. False

QUIZ ANSWERS

1. C – John Tait Robertson

2. B – False

3. C – Ted Drake

4. A – AC Milan

5. B – Rafael Benítez

6. D – Ruud Gullit

7. A – True

8. C – 5

9. A – David Webb

10. A – Inter Milan

11. B – José Mourinho

12. B – False

13. D – Frank Lampard

14. C – Atlético Madrid

15. D – 14

16. A – True

17. C – 8

18. C – André Villas-Boas

19. B – 6

20. A – True

DID YOU KNOW?

1. Chelsea has had just over 35 known different full-time and interim managers. The first was John Tait Robertson in 1905, and the most recent is Thomas Tuchel, who was appointed in January 2021 when Frank Lampard was fired. Ron Stuart, José Mourinho, and Guus Hiddink each had two stints as the club's manager, while the rest were hired and fired just once each.

2. David Calderhead of Scotland has been the club's longest-serving manager, as he held the position from August 1, 1907, to May 8, 1933, and was in charge for nearly 1,000 games. Former playing great Danny Blanchflower of Northern Ireland was the team's shortest-reigning full-time boss, as he was in charge for just over 30 contests between December 14, 1978, and September 11, 1979.

3. The Blues boss who first won a major trophy was Ted Drake of England, who held the job between June 1, 1952, and September 30, 1961. Drake guided his players to the First Division title in 1954-55. Dave Sexton of England was in charge of the club when it won its first major title in Europe, the UEFA Cup Winners' Cup in 1970-71, as he was in charge from October 23, 1967, to October 3, 1974.

4. José Mourinho of Portugal won the most domestic trophies with the Blues, as he captured three Premier League titles and League Cups as well as an FA Cup and

a FA Community Shield. He held the position from June 2, 2004, to September 19, 2007, and again between June 3, 2013, and December 17, 2015. Mourinho started his managerial career with Benfica. He won the European Champions League with Inter Milan and Porto as well as league championships in four different European nations at Porto, Chelsea, Inter Milan, and Real Madrid.

5. When it comes to being honored with major awards, the IFFHS World's Best Club Coach was won by José Mourinho in 2005, and he was runner-up in 2006, while Roberto Di Matteo was runner-up in 2012. Mourinho was named Premier League Manager of the Season for 2004-05, 2005-06, and 2014-15, while Antonio Conte took the honor in 2016-17.

6. Rafael Benítez of Spain held the manager's job from November 21, 2012, to May 27, 2013, as the interim boss when Roberto Di Matteo was fired. His appointment was unpopular with some Chelsea supporters since Benítez formerly managed Liverpool and had made disparaging comments about the Blues in the past. In fact, he received a rather hostile reception after being introduced to the Stamford Bridge crowd during his first home game on November 25, 2012, a 0-0 draw with Manchester City. However, he did lead the team to the Europa League crown in 2012-13.

7. Rafael Benítez and José Mourinho made their English debuts in 2004-05, Benítez at Liverpool and Mourinho at

Chelsea, and they both liked to play mind games. The clubs met often with the managers getting on each other's nerves. Mourinho usually held the upper hand during league contests, while Benítez came out on top in the Community Shield, FA Cup, and European Champions League. Benítez told the media that Chelsea was boring, while Mourinho asked Benítez what he had won? Benítez was later chided by Mourinho for winning the Europa League with Chelsea while his players had captured the Champions League. Mourinho then took over the club when Benítez was let go.

8. José Mourinho didn't get along with Frank Rijkaard, either, when the Dutchman managed Barcelona. Mourinho dismissed Rijkaard's managerial record in the media, claiming he had an empty trophy cabinet while Mourinho's was full. Things boiled over in a 2005 European Champions League match when Barcelona edged the Blues 2-1 in Spain. Chelsea's Didier Drogba was ejected in the second half, and Mourinho claimed this was due to Rijkaard complaining to referee Anders Frisk at halftime. Frisk then received death threats from some Chelsea fans and retired soon after. Chelsea won 4-2 in the home leg, and Rijkaard tried to get at Mourinho in the tunnel following the match.

9. Carlo Ancelotti took over from June 1, 2009, to May 22, 2011, and was the team's fourth full-time boss in just 21 months, following José Mourinho, Avram Grant, and Luiz Felipe Scolari. He led the side to the league title and FA

Cup in 2009-10, becoming the first Italian manager to win the Premier League crown. Ancelotti was fired following Chelsea's final game of the season in 2011 after finishing as runner-up. He posted 67 wins, 20 draws, and 22 losses in 109 games and, at the time, held the third-highest winning percentage in Premier League history, behind José Mourinho and Sir Alex Ferguson.

10. The club's first non-British manager was former Dutch international playing legend Ruud Gullit, who had played for Chelsea between 1995 and 1998. In fact, Gullit was player-manager from 1996 to 1998 before hanging up his boots to concentrate on managing. He took over the team when Glenn Hoddle, who was also a player-manager, left to take over as England's manager. Gullit led the squad to an FA Cup triumph in 1996-97 for their first major trophy in 26 years. He was eventually fired and replaced by Gianluca Vialli, with Gullit then taking over as manager at Newcastle United.

CHAPTER 4:

GOALTENDING GREATS

QUIZ TIME!

1. Who played between the posts in Chelsea's first-ever Premier League match?

    a. Frode Grodås
    b. Dmitri Kharine
    c. Dave Beasant
    d. Kevin Hitchcock

2. Peter Bonetti has made the second most appearances in all competitions for Chelsea.

    a. True
    b. False

3. Who backed up Thibaut Courtois for 17 matches in the 2015-16 campaign?

    a. Petr Čech
    b. Asmir Begović
    c. Mark Schwarzer
    d. Ross Turnbull

4. Which keeper made 21 appearances in the 1996-97 Premier League?

    a. Craig Forrest
    b. Frode Grodås
    c. Nick Colgan
    d. Ed de Goey

5. How many clean sheets did Petr Čech keep with Chelsea?

    a. 140
    b. 154
    c. 228
    d. 271

6. What was Peter Bonetti's nickname?

    a. The Wizard
    b. The Gymnast
    c. Mr. Tiger
    d. The Cat

7. Eddie Niedzwiecki severely injured a ligament in his knee, forcing him to retire at the age of 28.

    a. True
    b. False

8. Who made 36 domestic league appearances in the 2002-03 season?

    a. Ed de Goey
    b. Carlo Cudicini
    c. Mark Bosnich
    d. Neil Sullivan

9. Which keeper recorded 14 clean sheets in the 2018-19 Premier League?

   a. Asmir Begović
   b. Thibaut Courtois
   c. Willy Caballero
   d. Kepa

10. Kevin Hitchcock played for which club before joining Chelsea?

    a. Northampton Town
    b. Watford FC
    c. Mansfield Town
    d. Nottingham Forrest

11. How many clean sheets did Ed de Goey post in the 1999-2000 Premier League?

    a. 9
    b. 13
    c. 16
    d. 17

12. Thibaut Courtois won the Best FIFA Men's Goalkeeper award in 2018.

    a. True
    b. False

13. Who is the oldest player to make an appearance for Chelsea's first team, at the age of 41 years and 218 days?

    a. Ed de Goey
    b. Henrique Hilário

c. Mark Schwarzer

d. Willy Caballero

14. How many appearances did Peter Bonetti make for Chelsea in all competitions?

    a. 729

    b. 675

    c. 622

    d. 590

15. Carlo Cudicini was originally loaned to Chelsea by which club?

    a. S.S. Lazio

    b. A.S.D. Castel di Sangro Calcio

    c. Paris Saint-Germain

    d. AC Milan

16. Chelsea's first-ever keeper, William Foulke, played four seasons with the squad.

    a. True

    b. False

17. Which club did Edouard Mendy play for before joining Chelsea in 2021?

    a. Stade Rennais FC

    b. Olympique de Marseille B

    c. Stade Reims

    d. AS Cherbourg

18. How many times did Petr Čech win the Premier League's Golden Glove award with Chelsea?

a. 4

b. 1

c. 5

d. 3

19. How many clean sheets did Petr Čech post in 2004-05 to set a Premier League record?

    a. 27

    b. 24

    c. 21

    d. 18

20. Mark Schwarzer made 109 appearances for the Australian national team.

    a. True

    b. False

QUIZ ANSWERS

1. C – Dave Beasant

2. A – True

3. B – Asmir Begović

4. B – Frode Grodås

5. C – 228

6. D – The Cat

7. A – True

8. B – Carlo Cudicini

9. D – Kepa

10. C – Mansfield Town

11. C – 16

12. A – True

13. C – Mark Schwarzer

14. A – 729

15. B – A.S.D. Castel di Sangro Calcio

16. B – False

17. A – Stade Rennais FC

18. D – 3

19. B – 24

20. A – True

DID YOU KNOW?

1. Chelsea's first-ever keeper was William "Fatty" Foulke, and although he played just one season, he's still one of the club's famous players. He signed from Sheffield United for £50 after winning two FA Cups there and was a giant at 6 feet, 4 inches tall and over 300 lbs. He was a very agile and athletic keeper, though, and saved a penalty kick in the club's first competitive match. Foulke played 35 games for the team and conceded 28 goals. The captain missed six games that season, and the club allowed 17 goals in his absence. Foulke moved to Bradford City in 1906 and passed away from cirrhosis at the age of 41 in 1916.

2. Compared to William Foulke, Jim Molyneux was rather small at 5 feet, 9 inches tall but that didn't stop him from performing heroics in goal. He was signed in 1910 from Stockport County as a backup to Jack Whitley. However, he soon earned the number one job and held it for 12 years. The agile Englishman was known as "Molly" and played in the team's first FA Cup final, a 3-0 loss to Sheffield United in 1914-15. He retired in 1923 after recording 77 clean sheets in 239 official games.

3. Australian international Mark Schwarzer was as steady as they come, as he posted just over 150 clean sheets in the Premier League in 515 outings from 1997 to 2016.

Schwarzer became the first non-British player to appear in 500 Premier League matches and was the oldest player to represent both Chelsea and Leicester City in the Premier League. He joined the Blues in July 2013 from Fulham on a free transfer and played for the team when he was 41 years and 218 days old. Schwarzer played just a dozen times for the club but will go down in history as one of the best keepers in the Premier League.

4. Petr Čech played with the side from 2004 to 2015 after joining from Rennes for a then-record fee for a keeper of £7 million. He became the most-capped player for the Czech Republic at 124 while being named that nation's Player of the Year a record nine times. He won 15 team trophies and several individual awards with Chelsea while setting numerous club and league records. He played 494 times with the Blues and holds the team record for clean sheets at 228, including 24 in the 2004-05 league. Čech left for Arsenal in 2015 for £10 million but returned to Chelsea in 2019 as a technical adviser and emergency keeper.

5. It's hard to believe Peter "The Cat" Bonetti played just seven times for England while playing for Chelsea from 1960 to 1975 and 1976 to 1979. He left on a free transfer in 1975 to play in America before returning to the Blues. Bonetti appeared in 729 games to rank second on the club's all-time appearance list after Ron Harris, and he recorded 208 clean sheets. He also conceded one goal or less in 66.6% of his outings with Chelsea. Bonetti won five

trophies with the team as well as the FA Youth Cup in 1959-60 and helped the club out as a goalkeeping coach after retiring.

6. Carlo Cudicini originally arrived at Chelsea on a season-long loan from Castel di Sangro before being bought outright for £160,000. This turned out to be one of the best bargains in club history, as the Italian's penalty-saving skills and reflexes helped Cudicini capture the Player of the Year award in 2002. He played 216 times for the side and kept 101 clean sheets while winning two FA and League Cups and two FA Community Shields. Cudicini left for Tottenham Hotspur in January 2009 on a free transfer, only to return in 2016 as a Chelsea ambassador and coach.

7. English-born Sam Millington was signed from Wellington in 1926 just after turning 30 years old and helped Chelsea earn promotion to the top flight in 1929-30. He kept 14 clean sheets that season and played all but four games. Known for wearing a flat cap, Millington went on to appear in 245 games in a span of six years and posted 78 clean sheets. He had to hang up his boots due to injury in 1932 but remains one of the team's top performers between the posts.

8. After a shaky start with the Blues in 1997, Dutch international Ed de Goey settled down and helped the team win the League Cup and UEFA Cup Winners' Cup in his first season. He then helped the side capture the

1998 UEFA Super Cup, the 1999-2000 FA Cup, and the 2000 FA Charity Shield. De Goey set a then-club record for appearances in 1999-2000 at 59 and the 6-foot, 6-inch goalie was one of the team's tallest ever players. He contributed 73 clean sheets in 179 games before joining Stoke City in 2003.

9. English international Vic Woodley played with the outfit from 1931 to 1945, with his career being interrupted by World War II. Before the conflict began, he played 19 straight games for England as the nation's undisputed number one. He signed with Chelsea in 1930 from Windsor & Eton and played 272 times. His consistency and skills kept the team in the top flight during a difficult period. Woodley posted 60 clean sheets before leaving for Derby County.

10. Belgian international Thibault Courtois was signed from Genk in 2011 and loaned to Atlético Madrid a few weeks later. He didn't return to Chelsea until 2014-15 when he took over the starting job from Petr Čech. Courtois helped the team hoist the Premier League and League Cup double that season. He won the league again two years later, as well as the division's Golden Glove award for the most clean sheets, with 16. His final game with Chelsea was a 1-0 triumph over Manchester United in the 2017-18 FA Cup final. He then left for Real Madrid with 58 clean sheets to his name in 154 games.

CHAPTER 5:

DARING DEFENDERS

QUIZ TIME!

1. Ricardo Carvalho left which Portuguese club to join Chelsea?

    a. S.L. Benfica

    b. C.S. Marítimo

    c. Rio Ave FC

    d. FC Porto

2. Gary Cahill played the most minutes for Chelsea in the 2016-17 Premier League season.

    a. True

    b. False

3. Which defender appeared in 312 games with the club and notched 16 goals?

    a. Tommy Logan

    b. Graeme Le Saux

    c. Steve Clarke

    d. Eddie McCreadie

4. Steve Clarke left which Scottish club to join the Blues?

   a. Aberdeen FC

   b. St. Mirren FC

   c. Livingston FC

   d. Rangers FC

5. Who played 4,303 minutes in all competitions in 2010-11?

   a. Branislav Ivanović

   b. Bosingwa

   c. John Terry

   d. Ashley Cole

6. How many goals did Frank Leboeuf score in the 1997-98 Premier League?

   a. 3

   b. 8

   c. 2

   d. 5

7. Before joining Chelsea, Marcel Desailly won the 1998 FIFA World Cup with France.

   a. True

   b. False

8. Who scored four goals in the 2019-20 Premier League?

   a. Kurt Zouma

   b. Antonio Rüdiger

   c. Marcos Alonso

   d. César Azpilicueta

9. Which player tallied seven assists in the 2002-03 Premier League?

   a. Graeme Le Saux
   b. Mario Melchiot
   c. William Gallas
   d. Robert Huth

10. Which player had five goals in the 2012-13 Premier League?

   a. John Terry
   b. Branislav Ivanović
   c. Ashley Cole
   d. David Luiz

11. How many appearances did John Terry make in all competitions for Chelsea?

   a. 588
   b. 659
   c. 717
   d. 732

12. Frank Sinclair was the only defender to be shown a red card in the 1992-93 Premier League.

   a. True
   b. False

13. Which defender played 211 games with Chelsea without scoring a goal?

   a. John Harris
   b. Stan Willemse

c. John Sillett

d. Allan Craig

14. Which player scored four goals in the 1999-2000 Premier League?

    a. Frank Leboeuf

    b. Dan Petrescu

    c. Bernard Lambourde

    d. Jon Harley

15. How many goals did William Gallas score in the 2002-03 domestic league?

    a. 6

    b. 4

    c. 7

    d. 2

16. Wayne Bridge scored 27 goals in all competitions for Chelsea.

    a. True

    b. False

17. Who was shown six yellow cards in the 2016-17 domestic league?

    a. David Luiz

    b. Gary Cahill

    c. Marcus Alonso

    d. Branislav Ivanović

18. How many appearances did William Gallas make for Chelsea in all competitions?

a. 44

b. 183

c. 212

d. 225

19. How many yellow cards was Ricardo Carvalho shown in all competitions in 2007-08?

a. 5

b. 9

c. 12

d. 16

20. Branislav Ivanović played in all 38 matches in the 2013-14 Premier League season.

a. True

b. False

QUIZ ANSWERS

1. D – FC Porto

2. B – False

3. B – Graeme Le Saux

4. B – St. Mirren FC

5. D – Ashley Cole

6. D – 5

7. A – True

8. C – Marcos Alonso

9. A – Graeme Le Saux

10. B – Branislav Ivanović

11. C – 717

12. A – True

13. D – Allan Craig

14. B – Dan Petrescu

15. B – 4

16. B – False

17. A – David Luiz

18. D – 225

19. C – 12

20. B – False

DID YOU KNOW?

1. English international Gary Cahill joined from Bolton Wanderers in January 2012 and made a name for himself as a dependable center-back with great aerial and tackling abilities. The former captain helped the team win the European Champions League and the FA Cup in his first campaign with the Blues. He added six more trophies to his cabinet before leaving for Crystal Palace in 2019 and contributed 25 goals in his 290 appearances. Cahill was named to the Professional Footballers' Association Team of the Year three times.

2. In two stints with Chelsea, Graeme Le Saux played 312 games and notched 16 goals. He started as a winger with the team before moving to left-back. The English international kicked off his career at Stamford Bridge in 1989 and, in 1993, moved to Blackburn Rovers, where he won the Premier League in 1994-95. He returned to Chelsea in 1997 for £5 million, which made him the most expensive English defender at the time. He helped the team win five trophies but missed the UEFA Cup Winners' Cup and FA Cup triumphs due to injury. Le Saux left for Southampton in 2003 and later became a television soccer broadcaster.

3. Ricardo Carvalho of Portugal was one of manager José Mourinho's favorite players; he played for Mourinho with

three different clubs. The center-back won several trophies with his boss at Porto and was named the Portuguese League's Player of the Year before joining Mourinho at Stamford Bridge in 2004. With Chelsea, Carvalho's play helped the side win eight pieces of silverware while he contributed 11 goals in 210 games. He also earned the Chelsea Players' Player of the Year nod in 2008 and was named to the FIFA FIFPro World XI three times with the club. Carvalho left in 2010 for Real Madrid, where Mourinho was the manager.

4. Serbian international Branislav Ivanović was a versatile defender who arrived at the club in 2008 from Lokomotiv Moscow and stayed for nine years. He appeared in 377 contests and racked up 34 goals, tied for second on the team's scoring list for defenders. Ivanović helped the squad haul in 11 trophies before the vice-captain joined Zenit St. Petersburg in February 2017. He was also named to the PFA Team of the Year and Serbian Player of the Year twice with Chelsea, as well as the UEFA Europa League final Man of the Match in 2013 and to the UEFA Champions League Team of the Season in 2014-15.

5. David Webb played one game shy of 300 for the Blues. He could play just about anywhere on the pitch, with the back line being the most common. He arrived in 1968 from Southampton for £60,000 and was a key member of the team, helping it win the 1969-70 FA Cup and 1970-71 European Cup Winners' Cup. Webb wore every number with the side from 1 to 12 at least once, except for number

51

11. He even went into goal in a December 1971 game against Ipswich Town and posted a clean sheet. He could also score, as he netted 33 times with Chelsea. This included the winner in the 1970 FA Cup final replay. Webb joined Queens Park Rangers in 1974 but returned to the Blues in February 1993 for a brief spell as interim manager.

6. As of February 2021, former defender Steve Clarke was managing the Scottish national team, a side he once played for. He also played 421 times for Chelsea after arriving from St. Mirren in 1987, and he hung up his boots with the team 11 years later. Clarke helped the squad snag the 1996-97 FA Cup, the 1997-98 League Cup, and the 1997-98 UEFA Cup Winners' Cup. He was named to Chelsea's centenary team best 11 at right-back in 2005 when the club celebrated its 100th birthday. Clarke returned to the club as a youth team coach and served as assistant manager under José Mourinho and Avram Grant from 2004 to 2008.

7. English international left-back Ashley Cole joined Chelsea from Arsenal in 2006 in a controversial move that saw William Gallas leave Stamford Bridge for Arsenal. Cole was already well established as one of the league's best defenders and had helped Arsenal win several trophies. He went on to make 338 appearances with Chelsea while posting seven goals and 38 assists. Cole also added more silverware to his collection as he helped the team win trophies while picking up several individual awards as

well. He left in 2014 to join Roma and played 107 times for England.

8. With 217 games under his belt from 2004 to 2013, Portuguese international Paulo Ferreira was rock solid for Chelsea. He arrived from Porto for £13.2 million along with his former manager José Mourinho and teammate Ricardo Carvalho. He helped the outfit win an even dozen trophies including three Premier League titles, four FA Cups, a League Cup, the Europa League, and the European Champions League. After hanging up his boots, Ferreira remained with the club as a technical coach for loan players.

9. Tommy Law of Scotland played his entire pro career with the Blues from 1926 to 1938, appearing in 318 games and registering 19 goals, with 16 of those coming via penalty kicks. He signed from local junior club Bridgeton Waverley at the age of 18 and proved to be a reliable, hard-working left-back throughout his career. In 1932, Law was offered more than double his salary to play in France but turned it down. Although he could be depended on game after game, he played just twice for Scotland.

10. After spending his youth career with Chelsea, Colin Pates made his first-team debut in 1979 at the age of 18. He became the club captain at 22 and remained with the squad until 1988 when he was sold to Charlton Athletic for £430,000. He made 346 outings for the Blues and

helped out with 10 goals. He later played for Arsenal and Brighton & Hove Albion but retired from the top-level due to injury and became a coach. Pates was a calm, composed central defender who displayed excellent leadership qualities both on and off the pitch.

CHAPTER 6:

MAESTROS OF THE MIDFIELD

QUIZ TIME!

1. Who won the Premier League Player of the Season award for 2004-05?

    a. Frank Lampard

    b. Claude Makélélé

    c. Anthony Grant

    d. Aleksey Smertin

2. Chelsea has had five different players make the FIFPro XI team as of 2020.

    a. True

    b. False

3. How many yellow cards was Jorginho shown in the 2019-20 Premier League?

    a. 0

    b. 5

    c. 8

    d. 10

4. Who scored five goals in the 1992-93 Premier League?

    a. Eddie Newton

    b. Andy Townsend

    c. Dennis Wise

    d. Gareth Hall

5. Which player tallied nine goals in all competitions in 1997-98?

    a. Roberto Di Matteo

    b. Dennis Wise

    c. Gustavo Poyet

    d. Jody Morris

6. How many goals did Frank Lampard score in the 2003-04 domestic league?

    a. 12

    b. 7

    c. 15

    d. 10

7. Cesc Fàbregas won the Premier League Player of the Season award for 2016-17.

    a. True

    b. False

8. Which player scored three goals in the 2017-18 Premier League?

    a. Davide Zappacosta

    b. Tiémoué Bakayoko

    c. Victor Moses

    d. Cesc Fàbregas

9. How many goals did Terry Venables score in all competitions for Chelsea?

    a. 46
    b. 31
    c. 25
    d. 14

10. How many goals did Claude Makélélé notch with the Blues?

    a. 7
    b. 23
    c. 2
    d. 14

11. How many appearances did John Hollins make in all competitions for Chelsea?

    a. 417
    b. 458
    c. 520
    d. 592

12. Frank Lampard made the fourth most appearances in all competitions for Chelsea as of 2020.

    a. True
    b. False

13. Which player was shown 11 yellow cards in all competitions in 2000-01?

    a. Dennis Wise
    b. Samuele Dalla Bona

c. Judy Morris

d. Slaviša Jokanović

14. Who won the Premier League Player of the Season award in 2014-15?

a. Cesc Fàbregas

b. John Obi Mikel

c. Eden Hazard

d. N'Golo Kanté

15. Which player scored four goals in the 2006-07 Premier League?

a. Nijtap Geremi

b. Michael Ballack

c. John Obi Mikel

d. Michael Essien

16. Roberto Di Matteo was the only Blues player to receive a red card in all competitions in 1998-99.

a. True

b. False

17. Which player notched four goals in the 2018-19 domestic league?

a. Pedro

b. Eden Hazard

c. Willian

d. N'Golo Kanté

18. How many appearances did Frank Lampard make in all competitions?

a. 485

b. 570

c. 648

d. 663

19. Who recorded 19 assists in the 2014-15 Premier League?

a. Nemanja Matić

b. John Obi Mikel

c. Ramires

d. Cesc Fàbregas

20. Juan Mata earned 20 assists in the 2012-13 domestic league.

a. True

b. False

QUIZ ANSWERS

1. A – Frank Lampard

2. B – False

3. D – 10

4. A – Eddie Newton

5. A – Roberto Di Matteo

6. D – 10

7. B – False

8. C – Victor Moses

9. B – 31

10. C – 2

11. D – 592

12. A – True

13. A – Dennis Wise

14. C – Eden Hazard

15. B – Michael Ballack

16. B – False

17. D – N'Golo Kanté

18. C – 648

19. D – Cesc Fàbregas

20. B – False

DID YOU KNOW?

1. Vinnie Jones is widely known as a Hollywood actor and part-time singer these days, but he used to be one of the most unpredictable and toughest players of all time. Jones earned his reputation with Wimbledon when the team was known as the "Crazy Gang," and he joined the Blues in 1991 from Sheffield United for £575,000. He played 52 matches with seven goals, and, surprisingly, he received just three yellow cards during his stint. The English-born Jones played nationally for Wales and picked up 12 red cards during his pro career, once receiving a yellow card just three seconds after kickoff. Jones returned to Wimbledon in 1992 when the Premier League debuted.

2. Christian Pulisic was one of America's top prospects while playing with Dortmund and held the Bundesliga record being the youngest player to score twice, when he was 17 years and 218 days old. He also became the youngest foreign-born player to score in the league. Pulisic exhibits technical skills, versatility, and intelligence on the pitch. He was acquired by Chelsea in January 2019 but remained at Dortmund on loan. The reported £57.6 million fee was the most paid for an American player and the fourth highest for Chelsea. Pulisic has endured some injury problems with the Blues, but, as of February 2021, he had played in 55 games and notched 13 goals.

3. Spanish international playmaker Juan Mata arrived at Chelsea in 2011 from Valencia and scored 33 times in 135 matches. He helped the team win an FA Cup, a Europa League title, and a European Champions League crown. Mata was voted the squad's Player of the Year for 2011-12 and 2012-13 and the Chelsea Players' Player of the Year for 2012-13 and was named to the PFA Team of the Year for 2012-13. All good things come to an end, though, as Mata was sold to Manchester United in January 2014 and was still there as of February 2021.

4. Claude Makélélé was a French international who was born in Zaire and joined Chelsea in 2003 from Real Madrid. He scored just twice in 217 appearances but still contributed a great deal on the pitch. He helped the side capture the Premier League in 2004-05 and 2005-06, the FA Cup in 2006-07, and the League Cup in 2004-05 and 2006-07. The defensive midfielder used his energy, intelligence, and diligence to succeed by breaking up attacks and leading counterattacks. Makélélé left for Paris Saint-Germain in 2008 but returned to the Blues in 2019 as a technical mentor and youth coach.

5. Another prominent box-to-box Chelsea midfielder was Ghanaian international Michael Essien, who contributed 25 goals in his 256 appearances despite several serious injuries. He joined the team from Lyon in 2005 for a reported £24.4 million, which made him the club's most expensive signing at the time. He helped the side capture a pair of Premier League titles as well as three FA Cups, a

League Cup, and the European Champions League. He was named Chelsea's Player of the Year for 2007 and twice won the club's Goal of the Season award. Essien was loaned to Real Madrid in 2012 and signed with AC Milan in 2013-14.

6. Not known for his scoring prowess, Nigerian international John Obi Mikel was a regular with the Blues from 2006 to 2016 as a superb defensive midfielder. He managed just six goals in 372 games, but his play helped the side win two Premier League titles, four FA Cups, two League Cups, the European Champions League, and the Europa League. He was one of the team's anchors due to his unselfish and tidy work and was a key player in the 2012 Champions League squad. Mikel was named Chelsea Young Player of the Year in 2007 and 2008 and left on a free transfer to play in China in January 2017.

7. Former Arsenal skipper Cesc Fàbregas joined Chelsea in 2014 from Barcelona and notched 22 goals in 198 appearances while setting up dozens of others. He won two Premier League titles with the side, as well as an FA Cup and League Cup. Fàbregas won over supporters with his tremendous passing ability, which often split open the league's tightest defenses, and he earned 41 assists in the Premier League alone. The Spanish international left Stamford Bridge in January 2019 for Monaco, where he was still playing in 2020-21.

8. Central midfielder N'Golo Kanté joined from Leicester City in 2016 for a reported £32 million and was still with

the side in February 2021. He won the Premier League crown in 2016-17, the FA Cup in 2017-18, and the Europa League in 2018-19. The French international has won several individual awards with the team, including the PFA Players' Player of the Year, the Premier League Player of the Season, the FWA Footballer of the Year, and the Chelsea Players' Player of the Year all for 2016-17, and the Chelsea Player of the Year honor for 2018. The hardworking Kanté has appeared in over 200 games with the squad and shows no sign of slowing down.

9. Former Chelsea midfielder Damien Duff played an even 100 games for the Republic of Ireland and is now working with the team as a coach. The gifted Duff was a hard worker of the ball and netted 19 goals in his 125 appearances. He arrived in 2003 from Blackburn Rovers for a reported £17 million, and the natural left-footer usually played on the right side while Arjen Robben patrolled the left. Duff helped the outfit hoist two Premier League titles, an FA Community Shield, and a League Cup before leaving for Newcastle United for a reported fee of £5 million.

10. Scottish international Charlie Cooke joined Chelsea in 1966 from Dundee United for what was then a club-record £72,000. Six years later, he was sold to Crystal Palace for a reported £85,000. However, just 18 months after that, he returned to Stamford Bridge and remained until 1978 when he left to play in America. Chelsea was relegated in 1975 but, with Cooke's help, earned

promotion back to the top flight in 1976-77. During his two stints, Cooke notched 30 goals in 373 outings and won the FA Cup in 1969-70 and the European Cup Winners' Cup the next season.

CHAPTER 7:

SENSATIONAL STRIKERS & FORWARDS

QUIZ TIME!

1. Which player scored seven goals in the club's inaugural Premier League season?

   a. Neil Shipperley

   b. Tony Cascarino

   c. Robert Fleck

   d. John Spencer

2. Jimmy Floyd Hasselbaink once played the sport as a goalkeeper before converting to the outfield.

   a. True

   b. False

3. How many appearances did Roy Bentley make for the English national team?

   a. 30

   b. 23

   c. 12

   d. 8

4. Which player appeared in 37 matches in all competitions in 1996-97?

   a. Gianfranco Zola
   b. Gianluca Vialli
   c. Mark Hughes
   d. Craig Burley

5. George Hilsdon was given which nickname for his spectacular debut in 1906 and his sure-fire shot?

   a. The Cowboy of London
   b. Gung-Ho Hilsdon
   c. Iron Shoe
   d. Gatling Gun

6. Who was named to the FIFPro XI team in 2007?

   a. Salomon Kalou
   b. Didier Drogba
   c. Arjen Robben
   d. Shaun Wright-Phillips

7. Willian recorded 12 assists in the 2018-19 Premier League.

   a. True
   b. False

8. Who ranks third all-time in goals scored in all competitions as of 2020?

   a. Didier Drogba
   b. Kerry Dixon
   c. Peter Osgood
   d. George Mills

9. Who was the only player to be shown a red card in the 2000-01 Premier League?

   a. Jesper Grønkjær
   b. Mario Stanić
   c. Jimmy Floyd Hasselbaink
   d. Eiður Guðjohnsen

10. How many assists did Arjen Robben tally in the 2004-05 Premier League?

   a. 14
   b. 11
   c. 9
   d. 4

11. Who scored eight goals in the 2017-18 domestic league?

   a. Charly Musonda Jr.
   b. Pedro
   c. Alvaro Morata
   d. Olivier Giroud

12. George Hilsdon was the first player to score 100 goals for Chelsea in all competitions.

   a. True
   b. False

13. How many goals did Jimmy Greaves score for the youth team before being called up to the first-team squad?

   a. 114
   b. 95
   c. 83
   d. 72

14. Which player played 4,163 minutes in all competitions in 2008-09?

    a. Florent Malouda

    b. Franco Di Santo

    c. Didier Drogba

    d. Nicolas Anelka

15. Who scored 15 goals in all competitions in 2009-10?

    a. Deco

    b. Daniel Sturridge

    c. Florent Malouda

    d. Salomon Kalou

16. Didier Drogba scored 70 goals in 105 appearances for the Ivory Coast national team.

    a. True

    b. False

17. How many appearances did Kerry Dixon make in all competitions with Chelsea?

    a. 250

    b. 296

    c. 382

    d. 420

18. Which player posted eight goals in the 2019-20 Premier League?

    a. Callum Hudson-Odoi

    b. Michy Batshuayi

    c. Mason Mount

    d. Olivier Giroud

19. How many assists did Jimmy Floyd Hasselbaink record in 2002-03?

    a. 2

    b. 6

    c. 8

    d. 12

20. Didier Drogba earned 22 assists in all competitions in 2010-11.

    a. True

    b. False

QUIZ ANSWERS

1. D – John Spencer

2. A – True

3. C – 12

4. C – Mark Hughes

5. D – Gatling Gun

6. B – Didier Drogba

7. B – False

8. B – Kerry Dixon

9. C – Jimmy Floyd Hasselbaink

10. C – 9

11. C – Alvaro Morata

12. A – True

13. A – 114

14. D – Nicolas Anelka

15. C – Florent Malouda

16. B – False

17. D – 420

18. D – Olivier Giroud

19. C – 8

20. B – False

DID YOU KNOW?

1. Barry Bridges kicked off his career with the Blues from 1958 to 1966. He scored on his debut, but his 19 league goals in 1961-62 couldn't help the team from being relegated from the First Division. Bridges tallied 15 times in the league the next season as the squad earned promotion back to the top flight. In 1964-65, he scored 27 goals in all competitions to help the side capture the League Cup. Bridges notched 93 goals for Chelsea in just over 200 games and was then sold to Second Division Birmingham City in May 1966 for what was then a club-record £55,000.

2. Dutch international striker Jimmy Floyd Hasselbaink started his career as a goalkeeper before converting into a forward. He signed in May 2000 for a club-record £15 million from Atlético Madrid and proceeded to lead the Premier League in scoring during his first season with 23 goals. It was his second Golden Boot, as he had tallied 18 goals with Leeds United in 1998-99 to share the award. Hasselbaink scored 87 goals in just under 200 appearances with Chelsea before joining Middlesbrough in July 2004. In March 2004, he scored a hat-trick, becoming the first Chelsea player to score three goals in a game as a substitute.

3. Scottish international Hugh Gallacher joined the club in 1930 from Newcastle United for £10,000 and played until

1934 when he joined Derby County. He led the team in scoring in each of his four seasons and totaled 81 goals in 144 appearances. His second match for Chelsea took place in Newcastle and drew a record 68,386 fans for the northern club. Also, 55,000 came to see Gallacher's home debut against Manchester United and 74,000 filled Stamford Bridge when Arsenal came to visit. Gallacher was a huge draw, but the team failed to win anything while he was there.

4. Bob Whittingham contributed 31 league goals in 1910-11 to win the Second Division's Golden Boot. He had joined the club in April 1910 for £1,300 from Bradford City and chipped in with 80 goals in 129 outings. The team was relegated shortly after he arrived, but Whittingham helped it earn promotion to the First Division in 1911-12 by finishing as Second Division runner-up. He led the team in scoring in his first three seasons, but the First World War then broke out. He rejoined the club in 1919 and played just six more games before moving to Stoke City in 1919.

5. Before helping manage Chelsea between July 2018 and July 2019, Italian international Gianfranco Zola starred on the pitch for the team. He joined in 2006 for £4.5 million from Parma and was voted the Football Writers' Player of the Year in 1997. He played 312 times for the Blues and chipped in with 80 goals. The fans voted him Player of the Year twice, and in 2003, he won a club poll naming him Chelsea's greatest player ever. Zola left in 2003 to return

to Italy and play with Cagliari after helping Chelsea win six trophies.

6. Didier Drogba had a season to remember in 2009-10 when he scored 37 goals and set up 12 in 42 games. He won the Premier League Golden Boot with 29 goals and helped the team capture the league title. Unfortunately, Chelsea was eliminated from the European Champions League by eventual winners Inter Milan in the round-of-16 but hoisted the FA Cup for the second straight year to become the seventh English club to win the League and FA Cup double. In addition, Drogba was named to the Premier League Team of the Year for the second time and took home the Chelsea and African Player of the Year awards.

7. Spanish international Alvaro Morata scored 11 times in 52 games with Real Madrid before being sold to Juventus in 2014. After he won two league titles and two Coppa Italias with Juventus, Real Madrid reacquired him via their buy-back option. Morata remained red-hot and tallied 20 goals in 43 games when he returned, but Real then sold him to Chelsea in 2017 for a then-record fee of £60 million for the English side. He scored 24 goals in 72 games over two seasons before being loaned to Atlético Madrid, who eventually bought Morata for £58 million.

8. Like his father, Eiður Guðjohnsen was an Icelandic international. But unlike his father, Eiður racked up 78 goals for Chelsea in 263 contests. He arrived in June 2000 for £4.5 million from Bolton Wanderers and scored 13

times in his first season while used mainly as a substitute. He then formed a prolific partnership with Jimmy Floyd Hasselbaink for a couple of seasons. Guðjohnsen helped the team win back-to-back Premier League titles in 2004-05 and 2005-06 as well as the League Cup in 2004-05 and a pair of FA Charity/Community Shields before joining Barcelona in June 2006.

9. Ron Tindall arrived in 1953 from Camberley FC when he was still a teenager. He scored in his first-team debut two years later and then struck up a prolific striking partnership with Jimmy Greaves. Tindall notched 69 goals in 174 matches before being sold to West Ham United in November 1961. He was also an accomplished cricket player with Surrey from 1956 to 1966 and, after hanging up his boots and bat, moved to Australia, where he entered the world of football coaching.

10. Welsh international Mark Hughes was never a prolific scorer but displayed a terrific work ethic on the pitch. Nicknamed "Sparky," he arrived from Manchester United in 1995 after helping that club win 10 trophies. Hughes formed an effective partnership with Gianfranco Zola and helped the side win the 1996-97 FA Cup. He also won the 1997-98 League Cup and UEFA Cup Winners' Cup with the team before leaving for Southampton in 1998. Hughes contributed 39 goals in 123 games with the Blues.

CHAPTER 8:

NOTABLE TRANSFERS & SIGNINGS

QUIZ TIME!

1. How much did Chelsea reportedly pay for Ricardo Carvalho in 2004-05?

    a. €15 million
    b. €24 million
    c. €30 million
    d. €38 million

2. Chelsea signed William Foulke from Sheffield United for only £50.

    a. True
    b. False

3. Which Spanish club did Kepa play for before joining Chelsea in 2018-19?

    a. Celta Vigo
    b. SD Eibar
    c. Real Madrid
    d. Athletic Bilbao

4. How much was the transfer fee paid to Real Madrid for Claude Makélélé?

   a. €20 million
   b. €24 million
   c. €30 million
   d. €35 million

5. Chelsea signed Didier Drogba from which club in 2004-05?

   a. Paris Saint-Germain
   b. Galatasaray SK
   c. Olympique de Marseille
   d. EA Guingamp

6. Who is Chelsea's most expensive signing as of February 2021?

   a. Jorginho
   b. Kepa
   c. Christian Pulisic
   d. Fernando Torres

7. Steve Clarke was Chelsea's most expensive signing in 1986-87, costing the club €900,000.

   a. True
   b. False

8. For how much did Chelsea sign Andriy Shevchenko in 2006-07?

   a. €18 million
   b. €27 million

c. €38 million

d. €43 million

9. Which club did Peter Bonetti join in 1975?

    a. St. Louis Stars

    b. Dundee United

    c. Preston North End

    d. Cardiff City FC

10. Who was the most expensive player Chelsea sold in club history as of February 2021?

    a. Romelu Lukaku

    b. David Luiz

    c. Eden Hazard

    d. Juan Mata

11. Before joining the Blues, John Obi Mikel played for which club?

    a. Real Betis

    b. FC Twente

    c. FK Lyn

    d. Wycombe Wanderers

12. Chelsea sold Eden Hazard to Real Madrid for a fee of approximately €130 million.

    a. True

    b. False

13. Who was signed from West Ham United in 2001-02?

    a. Frank Lampard

    b. Emmanuel Petit

c. William Gallas

d. Sam Parkin

14. Which club did Dennis Wise play for before joining Chelsea?

a. West Bromwich Albion

b. Wimbledon FC

c. Queens Park Rangers

d. Newcastle United

15. How much did the club sell Romelu Lukaku for in 2014-15?

a. €46 million

b. €35 million

c. €31 million

d. €28 million

16. Chelsea sold John Terry to Aston Villa for a fee of €3 million.

a. True

b. False

17. Which club was Fernando Torres acquired from?

a. Paris Saint-Germain

b. Atlético Madrid

c. AC Milan

d. Liverpool FC

18. Which player was Chelsea's most expensive signing in 2013-14?

a. Willian

b. Nemanja Matić

c. Kurt Zouma

d. Samuel Eto'o

19. Which side did Chelsea sign Petr Čech from in 2004-05?

    a. FC Viktoria Plzen

    b. FK Chmel Blšany

    c. Stade Rennais

    d. AC Sparta Prague

20. Midfielder Juan Mata was sold to Manchester United.

    a. True

    b. False

QUIZ ANSWERS

1. C – €30 million

2. A – True

3. D – Athletic Bilbao

4. A – €20 million

5. C – Olympique de Marseille

6. B – Kepa

7. B – False

8. D – €43 million

9. A – St. Louis Stars

10. C – Eden Hazard

11. C – FK Lyn

12. B – False

13. A – Frank Lampard

14. B – Wimbledon FC

15. B – €35 million

16. B – False

17. D – Liverpool FC

18. A – Willian

19. C – Stade Rennais

20. A – True

DID YOU KNOW?

1. The top five reported transfer fees Chelsea has paid for players as of February 2021 are: midfielder Kai Havertz from Bayer 04 Leverkusen for £72 million in 2020-21; goalkeeper Kepa Arrizabalaga from Athletic Bilbao for £72 million in 2018-19; forward Alvaro Morata from Real Madrid for £59.4 million in 2017-18; forward Christian Pulisic from Borussia Dortmund for £57.6 million in 2018-19; and forward Fernando Torres from Liverpool for £52.65 million in 2010-11.

2. The top five transfer fees the club has received for players as of February 2021 are: forward Eden Hazard to Real Madrid for £103.5 million in 2019-20; forward Diego Costa to Atlético Madrid for £54 million in 2017-18; midfielder Oscar to Shanghai SIPG for £54 million in 2016-17; defender David Luiz to Paris Saint-Germain for £44.55 million in 2014-15; and midfielder Juan Mata to Manchester United for £40.26 million in 2013-14.

3. Chelsea has twice broken the record for the highest transfer fee paid by a British club. The club paid a then-record £39.49 million for Ukrainian international forward Andriy Shevchenko from AC Milan in June 2006. Chelsea then shelled out £52.65 million to Liverpool for Spanish international forward Fernando Torres in January 2011. In addition, Chelsea paid £72

million for Spanish international Kepa Arrizabalaga from Athletic Bilbao in August 2018 to set a new world record fee for a goalkeeper.

4. French international William Gallas handed a transfer request to the club manager in 2006, but José Mourinho rejected it. However, Gallas's contract was due to expire the following year, and he said he'd leave the club anyway because they weren't paying him enough. Chelsea released a statement claiming that Gallas said if he wasn't transferred he'd start scoring own goals. Gallas denied the accusation and called the club classless and petty. However, the player's wish was eventually granted when he was sent to Arsenal, with fellow defender Ashley Cole arriving at Chelsea as part of the transaction.

5. When Ashley Cole arrived at Chelsea from Arsenal in the William Gallas transfer in August 2006, Chelsea also paid its rivals £5 million. Cole was reportedly offered £55,000 a week by Arsenal in a new deal but knew Chelsea would pay him £90,000 per week. Cole and his agent had met Chelsea manager José Mourinho and CEO Peter Kenyon even though he was contracted to Arsenal and then re-signed with the Gunners. This resulted in all parties at the June 2005 meeting being fined heavily but then having them reduced following an appeal.

6. Dutch defender Winston Bogarde joined the Blues from Barcelona in 2000-01. However, he was soon glued to the bench after Claudio Ranieri replaced Gianluca Vialli as manager. Since Bogarde was making £40,000 a week, he

wasn't in any hurry to leave, even though Ranieri made it clear he didn't want the player. Bogarde remained at Stamford Bridge for the entire four years of his contract, but he was demoted to reserve and youth teams. He played just 11 times and retired after his contract expired.

7. In 2005, John Obi Mikel was playing with FK Lyn in Norway. Just after he turned 18 years of age, Manchester United announced they were buying him for £4 million in January 2006. FK Lyn claimed the deal was made with Mikel with no player agents involved. However, Chelsea claimed they made a deal with FK Lyn via Mikel's agents. FK Lyn denied this, while Mikel went to London in May 2005 to speak with Chelsea. Mikel claimed Man United pressured him into signing without his agents being present. United and FK Lyn complained to FIFA before all parties met to resolve the issue. Chelsea then paid £18 million for the player. After the director of FK Lyn was later found guilty of fraud and false claims, Chelsea wanted their money back, and their claim was settled out of court.

8. Chelsea paid £13.5 million to Anderlecht for Belgian international striker Romelu Lukaku in 2011 when he was just 18 years old. Lukaku rarely played, though, and was loaned to West Bromwich Albion in 2012 and Everton in 2013. Everton paid a loan fee of £3.15 million and then bought him outright for £31.82 million in July 2014. Lukaku was later sold from Everton to Manchester United in 2017 and then from United to Inter Milan two years

later. His transfer fees currently stand at £191.3 million, and he's Belgium's all-time national top scorer with 57 goals in 89 games. He's also won numerous individual awards but played just 15 games with Chelsea.

9. The Blues paid a reported £15.8 million to Parma in 2003 for Romanian international forward Adrian Mutu. He was a big hit with supporters after scoring four times in his first three games and notching 10 in 27 league outings. Manager José Mourinho didn't see eye to eye with him, though, and things spilled over when Mutu tested positive for cocaine. Chelsea claimed the player had breached his contract, released him, and took him to court to have his transfer fee reimbursed. Mutu was ordered to pay the club €17,173,990 plus 5% interest. He appealed the decision four times but to no avail and signed with Juventus in 2005.

10. Spanish international Fernando Torres was one of the hottest strikers in the world while playing for Liverpool from 2007 to 2011, with 65 goals in 102 league outings. He forced a transfer to Chelsea in January 2011 for a final total of £52.65 million, which was the most expensive in British soccer history at the time. It also turned out to be one of the worst, as Torres netted just 20 goals in 110 league contests for Chelsea. He did notch some important goals, but his total of 45 in 172 games in all competitions didn't sit well with the club, and he was loaned to Milan for two years in 2014, and he eventually rejoined Atlético Madrid.

CHAPTER 9:

ODDS & ENDS

QUIZ TIME!

1. How many matches did Chelsea win in 2016-17 for a club record?

   a. 32

   b. 30

   c. 27

   d. 25

2. Chelsea set the Premier League record for most goals scored at home in a single season in 2009-10.

   a. True

   b. False

3. Who is the youngest player to make an appearance for the side at 16 years and 138 days old?

   a. Ethan Ampadu

   b. John Sparrow

   c. Michael Woods

   d. Ian Hamilton

4. Which player scored five goals in a match on three separate occasions?

   a. Frank Lampard
   b. Bobby Tambling
   c. George Hilsdon
   d. Jimmy Greaves

5. Chelsea's biggest win in a League Cup match as of 2020 was a 7-0 victory against which club?

   a. Workington AFC
   b. Doncaster Rovers FC
   c. Manchester United
   d. Millwall FC

6. How many league matches did the Blues win when they were relegated in 1978-79?

   a. 5
   b. 8
   c. 3
   d. 10

7. Chelsea allowed only 12 goals against in the 2004-05 Premier League.

   a. True
   b. False

8. The team's highest-scoring draw in a league game as of 2020 was 5-5 against which club?

   a. Tottenham Hotspur
   b. Nottingham Forrest

c. Manchester City

d. West Ham United

9. Who scored the fastest goal in the squad's history in 12 seconds against Middlesbrough in 1970?

a. Keith Weller

b. Tommy Baldwin

c. John Boyle

d. Alan Hudson

10. What is the fewest goals Chelsea has scored in a Premier League season?

a. 46

b. 23

c. 37

d. 18

11. Which player didn't win a top-flight Golden Boot with the club?

a. Didier Drogba

b. Jimmy Greaves

c. Diego Costa

d. Nicolas Anelka

12. Chelsea went on a stretch of 46 matches without losing a game between 2004 and 2005.

a. True

b. False

13. The Blues hammered which side 9-1 for its biggest FA Cup victory?

a. Stoke City

b. Aston Villa

c. Peterborough United

d. Worksop Town

14. What is the most goals the club has scored in a Premier League season?

    a. 85

    b. 97

    c. 103

    d. 112

15. Who was the oldest player to make a first-team appearance with the club at 41 years and 218 days?

    a. Mark Schwarzer

    b. John Hollins

    c. Micky Droy

    d. Dennis Rofe

16. The most goals Chelsea has allowed in a domestic league season as of 2020 is 100.

    a. True

    b. False

17. How many points did Chelsea post in the 2004-05 Premier League?

    a. 82

    b. 87

    c. 95

    d. 98

18. Who was the first player to score four goals in a match in the Premier League era?

    a. Didier Drogba

    b. Jimmy Floyd Hasselbaink

    c. Frank Lampard

    d. Gianluca Vialli

19. Chelsea's biggest FA Cup defeat was 6-0 to which club?

    a. Brighton & Hove Albion

    b. Birmingham City

    c. Tottenham Hotspur

    d. Sheffield Wednesday

20. Chelsea lost just one Premier League match in the 2004-05 season.

    a. True

    b. False

QUIZ ANSWERS

1. B – 30

2. A – True

3. D – Ian Hamilton

4. D – Jimmy Greaves

5. B – Doncaster Rovers FC

6. A – 5

7. B – False

8. D – West Ham United

9. A – Keith Weller

10. A – 46

11. C – Diego Costa

12. B – False

13. D – Worksop Town

14. C – 103

15. A – Mark Schwarzer

16. A – True

17. C – 95

18. D – Gianluca Vialli

19. D – Sheffield Wednesday

20. A – True

DID YOU KNOW?

1. Since it was created, the club has redesigned the Chelsea crest several times throughout the years. The current Chelsea FC logo features a lion that is based on the lion in the civic coat of arms for the former Metropolitan Borough of Chelsea. Also, the club's official mascot is named Stamford the Lion, and his mascot partner is named Bridget the Lioness.

2. Stamford Bridge originally opened on April 28, 1877, and for 27 years, it hosted athletics meetings organized by the London Athletic Club. The stadium was originally planned to hold 100,000 fans, which would have made it the second-largest in England at the time behind the Crystal Palace stadium in south London. The venue's current capacity is 40,834, with the lowest attendance being 3,000 for a Chelsea versus Lincoln City clash in 1906.

3. Nicknamed "the Bridge," the highest official attendance at Stamford Bridge stands at 82,905 for a league encounter and London derby between Chelsea and Arsenal on October 12, 1935. The club is hoping to expand its current capacity to approximately 60,000 by the time the 2023-24 season kicks off. The venue was renovated in 1998 and was used by the London Monarchs NFL Europe team for

its home games in 1997. It has also hosted other types of events in the past, including greyhound racing.

4. In 2005, the club opened a museum named the Chelsea Museum/Centenary Museum to mark the 100th anniversary of Chelsea FC. Located in the former Shed Galleria, where visitors can explore the history of the team via video, memorabilia, and more. A new museum was opened at Stamford Bridge in June 2011 with interactive exhibits and is currently the largest soccer museum in London.

5. The team's away colors are typically all yellow or all white with blue trim. However, black or dark blue away kits have also been worn. In the 1966 FA Cup semifinal, the players wore black and blue stripes that were similar to the shirts worn by Inter Milan of Italy. Also, in the mid-1970s the team wore an away strip that featured red, white, and green similar to the one worn by the national team of Hungary in the 1950s. Several other away kits have also been worn over the years.

6. During the side's home games, Chelsea supporters often sing inspiring chants such as "Carefree," to the tune of "Lord of the Dance" but with the fans' own lyrics. Other songs sung include "Ten Men Went to Mow," "We All Follow the Chelsea," "Zigga Zagga," and "Celery."

7. Being located in London, Chelsea has natural derbies and rivalries against fellow London clubs, such as Arsenal, Tottenham Hotspur, Fulham, West Ham United, Queens

Park Rangers, Brentford, and Crystal Palace. The club also has a strong rivalry with Leeds United that dates back to the 1960s and 1970s. In addition, a rivalry with Liverpool has grown after the teams met several times in cup competitions, including the European Champions League.

8. On August 15, 1928, Chelsea and Arsenal became the first teams to place numbers on the back of their shirts. The club was the first in England to travel by airplane to a domestic away contest when they flew north to take on Newcastle United on April 19, 1957. Chelsea was also the first top-flight team in England to play a Sunday game when they met Stoke City on January 27, 1974.

9. Chelsea was the first British club to field 11 foreign-born players (non-British and -Irish) in its starting lineup when they did so against Southampton on December 26, 1999. The team was the first to win the FA Cup at the new Wembley Stadium, in May 2007, and was the last to hoist it at the old Wembley Stadium, in May 2000. Chelsea is also the only London-based club to win the European Cup/UEFA Champions League.

10. A song named "Blue is the Colour" was released in the UK before the 1971-72 League Cup final between Chelsea and Stoke City. The song was sung by all members of the club's first-team squad, and it rocketed up to number five on the British singles chart. Since then, the song has been used as an anthem by several other sports clubs including the Vancouver Whitecaps of MLS, with the name being

changed to "White is the Colour." Also, members of Chelsea teamed up with singer Graham McPherson in 1997 to sing "Blue Day," which reached number 22 in the singles charts. The squad then won the 1996-97 FA Cup 2-0 over Middlesbrough.

CHAPTER 10:

DOMESTIC COMPETITION

QUIZ TIME!

1. How many domestic trophies in all divisions has Chelsea won as of 2020?

    a. 16
    b. 18
    c. 21
    d. 25

2. Chelsea reached the FA Cup final in their first year competing for the trophy.

    a. True
    b. False

3. Which club did the Blues defeat to win their first FA Cup in 1970?

    a. Swansea City
    b. Sutton United
    c. Burnley FC
    d. Leeds United

4. Chelsea beat which team to win the 1965 Football League Cup final?

   a. Leicester City
   b. Aston Villa
   c. Birmingham City
   d. Norwich City

5. How many times has Chelsea won the FA Cup as of 2020?

   a. 3
   b. 5
   c. 8
   d. 13

6. Which season did the club win its first domestic league and FA Cup double?

   a. 1954-55
   b. 1996-97
   c. 2009-10
   d. 2016-17

7. Chelsea won its first Football League Cup thanks to an own goal by opposing player John Mortimer.

   a. True
   b. False

8. Chelsea won its first FA Community Shield final 3-0 against which club?

   a. Arsenal
   b. Newcastle United
   c. Wolverhampton Wanderers
   d. Manchester United

9. How many times have the Blues won the top-flight First Division/Premier League as of 2020?

   a. 6
   b. 8
   c. 5
   d. 10

10. Which player scored the winning goal for the team in the 2009 FA Cup final?

   a. Frank Lampard
   b. Didier Drogba
   c. Nicolas Anelka
   d. Michael Ballack

11. When did Chelsea win the First Division for the first time in club history?

   a. 1960-61
   b. 1954-55
   c. 1948-49
   d. 1909-10

12. The squad has been runner-up to the FA Community Shield nine times as of 2020.

   a. True
   b. False

13. Which side did Chelsea play in the 2014-15 Football League Cup final?

   a. Liverpool FC
   b. Derby County

c. Tottenham Hotspur

d. Manchester United

14. Which player was named man of the match in the 2000 FA Cup final?

a. Frank Leboeuf

b. John Terry

c. Dennis Wise

d. Ed de Goey

15. How many times has Chelsea won the Football League Cup as of 2020?

a. 3

b. 7

c. 2

d. 5

16. Chelsea has won the Second Division four times as of 2020.

a. True

b. False

17. Chelsea faced which club in the 2010 FA Cup final?

a. Portsmouth FC

b. Preston North End

c. Cardiff City

d. Southampton FC

18. How many FA Charity/Community Shields has the club won as of 2020?

a. 7

b. 3

c. 4

d. 6

19. Which club did Chelsea face in the 1997-98 Football League Cup final?

    a. Liverpool FC

    b. Ipswich Town

    c. Middlesbrough FC

    d. Arsenal

20. Chelsea won the Premier League in three consecutive seasons, from 2004-05 to 2006-07.

    a. True

    b. False

QUIZ ANSWERS

1. D – 25

2. B – False

3. D – Leeds United

4. A – Leicester City

5. C – 8

6. C – 2009-10

7. B – False

8. B – Newcastle United

9. A – 6

10. A – Frank Lampard

11. B – 1954-55

12. A – True

13. C – Tottenham Hotspur

14. C – Dennis Wise

15. D – 5

16. B – False

17. A – Portsmouth FC

18. C – 4

19. C – Middlesbrough FC

20. B – False

DID YOU KNOW?

1. Chelsea has won the First Division/Premier League six times as of 2010, along with eight FA Cups and five League Cups. The Charity/Community Shield has been captured on four occasions. In addition, the team has won a pair of Second Division titles.

2. Chelsea's top-flight titles were won in the following seasons: 1954-55, 2004-05, 2005-06, 2009-10, 2014-15, and 2016-17. The team was also runner-up in 2003-04, 2006-07, 2007-08, and 2010-11. The Second Division championship was captured in 1983-84 and 1988-89, while the squad finished as runner-up and earned promotion in 1906-07, 1911-12, 1929-30, 1962-63, and 1976-77.

3. The Football League/EFL Cup was won in 1964-65, 1997-98, 2004-05, 2006-07, and 2014-15, and the team placed as runner-up in 1971-72, 2007-08, and 2018-19. The FA Cup triumphs came in 1969-70, 1996-97, 1999-2000, 2006-07, 2008-09, 2009-10, 2011-12, and 2017-18. The Blues were also runners-up in 1914-15, 1966-67, 1993-94, 2001-02, 2016-17, and 2019-20.

4. Chelsea managed to win the FA Charity/Community Shield in 1955, 2000, 2005, and 2009. The club finished as runner-up in 1970, 1997, 2006, 2007, 2010, 2012, 2015, 2017, and 2018. Chelsea has been relegated from England's top flight (First Division) to the second tier (Second Division)

of soccer six times, in 1909-10, 1923-24, 1961-62, 1974-75, 1978-79, and 1987-88.

5. The club has pulled off half a dozen doubles so far, which consist of the following: League and FA Cup in 2009-10; League title and League Cup in 2004-05 and 2014-15; League Cup and European Cup Winners' Cup in 1997-98; FA Cup and League Cup in 2006-07; FA Cup and UEFA Champions League in 2011-12.

6. The biggest top-flight win for Chelsea was 8-0 over Wigan Athletic in 2010 and against Aston Villa in 2012. Their biggest top-flight setback was 8-1 against Wolverhampton Wanderers in 1953. The team went on a record run of 86 straight league matches without losing in the top flight between March 20, 2004, and October 26, 2008. This beat the old mark of 63 games, set by Liverpool between 1978 and 1980.

7. Chelsea holds the English record for the fewest goals allowed in a league campaign at 15 and the most clean sheets in a Premier League season with 25. Both of these marks were recorded in 2004-05. The team also posted a record six straight clean sheets from the start of a league season in 2005-06. Their streak of 11 consecutive away league victories in 2008 is also a top-flight record in England. The squad was the first Premier League side and first in the nation's top flight since 1962-63 to score at least 100 goals in a campaign, which they did in 2009-10 when they tallied 103 of them.

8. Chelsea players have won the Golden Boot to lead their division in scoring 10 times. Those to win it in the top flight were: 1958-59, Jimmy Greaves (33); 1960-61, Jimmy Greaves (41); 1984-85, Kerry Dixon (24); 2000-01, Jimmy Floyd Hasselbaink (23); 2006-07, Didier Drogba (20); 2008-09, Nicolas Anelka (19); 2009-10, Didier Drogba (29). Those who won it in the Second Division were: 1910-11, Bob Whittingham (31); 1962-63, Bobby Tambling (35); 1983-84, Kerry Dixon (28).

9. The club's record FA Cup win was 9-1 versus Worksop Town in the first round on January 11, 1908, and the biggest League Cup triumph was 7-0 versus Doncaster Rovers in the third round on November 16, 1960. Chelsea's biggest FA Cup defeat was 6-0 by Sheffield Wednesday in a second-round replay on February 5, 1913, while its worst League Cup loss was 6-2 by Stoke City in a third-round replay on October 22, 1974. The most League defeats in a season was 27 in the First Division in 1978-79, with the fewest league losses in a campaign being just one in the 2004-05 Premier League.

10. The Premier League Golden Glove is an annual award presented to the goalkeeper with the most clean sheets. Chelsea keepers have won the honor four times. They were Petr Čech in 2004-05 with 24; Petr Čech in 2009-10 with 17; Petr Čech in 2013-14 with 16; and Thibaut Courtois in 2017-18 with 16. Čech held the league record as of 2020 with 24 clean sheets in a single campaign.

CHAPTER 11:

EUROPE & BEYOND

QUIZ TIME!

1. How many international trophies has Chelsea won as of 2020?

   a. 4
   b. 6
   c. 10
   d. 13

2. The Inter-Cities Fairs Cup was the first international competition Chelsea competed for in 1958-59.

   a. True
   b. False

3. Despite qualifying for the inaugural European Cup in 1955, Chelsea withdrew from competition for which reason?

   a. Chelsea did not want to be the only team representing England.

b. Football League chairman Alan Hardaker influenced the club, believing that domestic trophies should take precedent.

c. Chelsea felt the competition was not worth the time.

d. Chelsea did not meet the minimum required players because of a problem securing passports for the players.

4. What was the first international trophy Chelsea won?

a. FIFA Club World Cup

b. European Cup

c. European Cup Winners' Cup

d. European Super Cup

5. What club did Chelsea face in the 2019 UEFA Super Cup final?

a. Liverpool FC

b. Atlético Madrid

c. Bayern Munich

d. Paris Saint-Germain

6. For which season did the Blues win their first UEFA Champions League trophy?

a. 1974-75

b. 1997-98

c. 2005-06

d. 2011-12

7. Chelsea was the first English club to win all four major UEFA trophies.

a. True

b. False

8. Which team did Chelsea defeat to win the 1971 European Cup Winners' Cup?

a. CSKA Sofia

b. Real Madrid

c. PSV Eindhoven

d. Club Brugge KV

9. Who scored the winning goal in the 1998 UEFA Super Cup final?

a. Tore André Flo

b. Gus Poyet

c. Celestine Babayaro

d. Marcel Desailly

10. How many times has Chelsea finished as runner-up in the UEFA Super Cup as of 2020?

a. 7

b. 5

c. 3

d. 1

11. Chelsea faced off against which squad in the 2012 FIFA Club World Cup final?

a. Auckland City FC

b. CF Monterrey

c. Al Ahly SC

d. SC Corinthians Paulista

12. Chelsea was eliminated by FC Barcelona in the 2007-08 UEFA Champions League final.

    a. True
    b. False

13. Which club did the Blues NOT face on their way to the 2011-12 UEFA Champions League final?

    a. S.S.C. Napoli
    b. FC Barcelona
    c. S.L. Benfica
    d. Olympique de Marseille

14. What was the final score of Chelsea's 2011-12 UEFA Champions League final victory?

    a. 6-5 on penalties
    b. 3-0
    c. 4-3 on penalties
    d. 2-1

15. Chelsea beat which outfit to win their first UEFA Europa League trophy?

    a. S.L. Benfica
    b. FC Basel
    c. S.S. Lazio
    d. Tottenham Hotspur

16. Eden Hazard scored the winning goal in the 2018-19 UEFA Europa League final.

    a. True
    b. False

17. Chelsea defeated which club 1-0 in the 1998 UEFA Cup Winners' Cup final?

   a. VfB Stuttgart
   b. Lokomotiv Moscow
   c. Real Betis
   d. Beerschot AC

18. Which club did Chelsea NOT play against on the way to the 2018 UEFA Europa League final?

   a. SK Slavia Prague
   b. Dynamo Kyiv
   c. Inter Milan
   d. Eintracht Frankfurt

19. The Blues downed which team to win its first UEFA Champions League trophy?

   a. Inter Milan
   b. Bayer Leverkusen
   c. AC Milan
   d. FC Bayern Munich

20. Chelsea is the only club to hold the UEFA Champions League and UEFA Europa League trophies at the same time.

   a. True
   b. False

QUIZ ANSWERS

1. B – 6

2. A – True

3. B – Football League chairman Alan Hardaker influenced the club, believing that domestic trophies should take precedent.

4. C – European Cup Winners' Cup

5. A – Liverpool FC

6. D – 2011-12

7. A – True

8. B – Real Madrid

9. B – Gus Poyet

10. C – 3

11. D – SC Corinthians Paulista

12. B – False

13. D – Olympique de Marseille

14. C – 4-3 on penalties

15. A – S.L. Benfica

16. B – False

17. A – VfB Stuttgart

18. C – Inter Milan

19. D – FC Bayern Munich

20. A – True

DID YOU KNOW?

1. Chelsea has won six major UEFA European trophies as of 2020. The club captured the European Champions League once and the UEFA Super Cup once and also hoisted the Europa League title and the UEFA Cup Winners' Cup twice each.

2. The club captured the European Champions League in 2011-12 and was runner-up in 2007-08. Chelsea hoisted the Europa League title in 2012-13 and 2018-19 and the European Cup Winners' Cup/UEFA Cup Winners' Cup in 1970-71 and 1997-98. The UEFA Super Cup was won in 1998, and the team was runner-up in 2012, 2013, and 2019. Chelsea has played in one FIFA Club World Cup as of 2020 and was runner-up in 2012.

3. Chelsea triumphed in the UEFA Europa League in 2012-13, becoming the first English club to win all four UEFA club trophies and the only club to hold both the European Champions League and Europa League titles at the same time.

4. Chelsea's biggest-ever victory in a competitive match came in the 1970-71 Cup Winners' Cup when the Blues thrashed Jeunesse Hautcharage of Luxembourg 13-0. Chelsea also beat Jeunesse Hautcharage 8-0 in the same competition for an aggregate score of 21-0, to set a record in European competition.

5. Chelsea's first European Champions League final took place in Moscow, Russia, in 2007-08 against fellow Premier League side Manchester United, making it the first time two English clubs battled each other in the final. Cristiano Ronaldo gave Man United the lead after 26 minutes, and Frank Lampard leveled the score just before the halftime whistle. Didier Drogba was sent off in extra time, and the match had to be settled by a penalty shootout with United winning 6-5 after seven kicks each.

6. The Blues returned to the Champions League final four years later, in 2011-12, when they faced Bayern Munich in Munich, Germany. This contest also went to a penalty shootout after ending in a 1-1 draw. Thomas Müller gave the hosts the lead with just seven minutes remaining, but Didier Drogba equalized it five minutes later. The Blues then won 4-3 in the shootout after five kicks each, with Chelsea goalkeeper Petr Čech saving the last two penalties. The keeper also saved an Arjen Robben penalty kick in extra time.

7. The first Europa League was won in 2012-13 when Chelsea edged Benfica of Portugal 2-1 in Amsterdam, Holland. Fernando Torres put the Blues ahead at the hour mark with Benfica's Óscar Cardozo converting a penalty in the 68th minute to tie the score. Branislav Ivanović then won it for the English side with a dramatic goal in the third minute of injury time. The second Europa League crown came in 2018-19 with a convincing 4-1 win over fellow London side Arsenal in Baku, Azerbaijan. Goals

came from Olivier Giroud in the 49th minute and Pedro in the 60th, with Eden Hazard scoring in the 65th and again seven minutes later via a penalty kick.

8. In the 1970-71 European Cup Winners' Cup, Chelsea played to a 1-1 draw with Real Madrid in Piraeus, Greece. Peter Osgood put Chelsea in front after 56 minutes, but Ignacio Zoco equalized in the final minute of play. The game ended 1-1 after extra time and was replayed two days later. This time, the Blues triumphed 2-1 with John Dempsey scoring in the 33rd minute followed by Peter Osgood six minutes later. Sebastián Fleitas then tallied for Real in the 75th minute.

9. Chelsea won the Cup Winners' Cup for the second time in 1997-98 as the European Cup Winners' Cup was renamed. They downed VfB Stuttgart of Germany 1-0 in Stockholm, Sweden, with Gianfranco Zola scoring the game's lone goal in the 71st minute. Dan Petrescu was sent off for Chelsea in the 85th minute with a straight red card, while Stuttgart's Gerhard Poschner received the same fate just before the final whistle.

10. The squad captured the UEFA Super Cup in Monaco in 1998 with a 1-0 win over Real Madrid, thanks to a Gus Poyet goal in the 83rd minute. However, Chelsea lost the 2012 edition 4-1 to Atlético Madrid in Monaco as well as the 2013 event when they were edged 5-4 in a penalty shootout following a 2-2 draw in Prague, Czech Republic. The score was level 1-1 after 90 minutes with Eden

Hazard giving Chelsea the lead in the third minute of extra time only to see Javi Martínez equalize just before the final whistle. They also lost the 2019 final 5-4 to Liverpool in a shootout in Istanbul, Turkey. This game also ended 1-1 after 90 minutes and 2-2 after 120.

CHAPTER 12:

TOP SCORERS

QUIZ TIME!

1. Who is the club's leading goal scorer in all competitions as of 2020?

    a. Bobby Tambling
    b. Roy Bentley
    c. Didier Drogba
    d. Frank Lampard

2. Jimmy Windridge was the first player to lead the team in scoring, with 20 goals in 1905-06.

    a. True
    b. False

3. Which player holds the club record for most hat-tricks in all competitions as of 2020?

    a. George Hilsdon
    b. Peter Osgood
    c. Jimmy Greaves
    d. Kerry Dixon

4. How many goals did Kerry Dixon score to lead the side in 1984-85?

   a. 36
   b. 24
   c. 18
   d. 13

5. Who led the club with 15 league goals in 2019-20?

   a. Christian Pulisic
   b. Olivier Giroud
   c. Willian
   d. Tammy Abraham

6. How many league goals did Jimmy Greaves tally in 1960-61 to win the Golden Boot?

   a. 26
   b. 37
   c. 41
   d. 49

7. Jimmy Greaves scored 13 hat-tricks in all competitions with Chelsea.

   a. True
   b. False

8. Who was the first Blues player to win the Golden Boot in the Premier League era?

   a. Didier Drogba
   b. Nicolas Anelka
   c. Arjen Robben
   d. Jimmy Floyd Hasselbaink

9. How many goals did Didier Drogba score to lead the Premier League in 2009-10?

    a. 32
    b. 23
    c. 35
    d. 29

10. Which two players led Chelsea with 14 goals each in all competitions in 1993-94?

    a. Eddie Newton and Neil Shipperley
    b. Zeke Rowe and Robert Fleck
    c. Gavin Peacock and Mark Stein
    d. John Spencer and Damian Matthew

11. Which player led the Second Division in goals in 1910-11?

    a. George Hilsdon
    b. Bob Whittingham
    c. Harold Halse
    d. Bob Thompson

12. George Hilsdon holds the club record for most goals scored in a match, with six.

    a. True
    b. False

13. How many goals did Jimmy Floyd Hasselbaink notch in the 2000-01 Premier League?

    a. 23
    b. 29
    c. 19
    d. 25

14. Which two players led Chelsea with nine goals each in the club's inaugural Premier League campaign?

    a. Dennis Wise and Andy Townsend
    b. Craig Burley and Nigel Spackman
    c. Michael Harford and Graham Stuart
    d. Tony Cascarino and David Hopkin

15. How many goals did Frank Lampard post in all competitions in his Chelsea career?

    a. 190
    b. 197
    c. 208
    d. 211

16. As of 2020, Chelsea has had 10 different players lead the First Division/Premier League in scoring.

    a. True
    b. False

17. After leaving Chelsea, Jimmy Greaves led the league in goals four times with which club?

    a. West Ham United
    b. Tottenham Hotspur
    c. Manchester City
    d. Fulham FC

18. Peter Osgood scored two goals in his first top-flight appearance for Chelsea against which club?

    a. Notts County FC
    b. Swindon Town

c. Aston Villa

d. Workington AFC

19. How many goals did Bobby Tambling score in domestic league matches for the team?

a. 129

b. 140

c. 164

d. 177

20. Hugh Gallacher led Chelsea in scoring in each of his four seasons with the club.

a. True

b. False

QUIZ ANSWERS

1. D – Frank Lampard

2. B – False

3. C – Jimmy Greaves

4. B – 24

5. D – Tammy Abraham

6. C – 41

7. A – True

8. D – Jimmy Floyd Hasselbaink

9. D – 29

10. C – Gavin Peacock and Mark Stein

11. B – Bob Whittingham

12. A – True

13. A – 23

14. C – Michael Harford and Graham Stuart

15. D – 211

16. B – False

17. B – Tottenham Hotspur

18. D – Workington AFC

19. C – 164

20. A – True

DID YOU KNOW?

1. English international midfielder Frank Lampard is the all-time leading scorer for Chelsea with 211 goals in 648 matches from 2001 to 2014. He tallied 147 times in league action, 38 times in domestic cups, 25 in Europe, and once in another competition. Lampard started his career with West Ham United in 1995, played with Swansea City on loan, and had stints with Manchester City and New York City FC after leaving Chelsea. He's currently the only midfielder to score 150 goals in the Premier League, and he managed Chelsea from July 4, 2019, until January 25, 2021. Lampard also won 13 team trophies and several individual awards with the Blues.

2. With 202 goals in 370 appearances and a team-high 162 in the league, forward Bobby Tambling ranks second on the team's all-time scoring list and held the top spot for 47 years until Frank Lampard broke it. He joined the Blues as a schoolboy at the age of 15 and marked his first-team debut in 1959 with a goal at the age of 17. Tambling left in 1970 for London neighbors Crystal Palace and now has a suite named after him at Stamford Bridge. He helped the side win the 1964-65 League Cup and was named to the team's greatest ever XI during the club's centenary celebrations.

3. English international striker Kerry Dixon left Reading for Chelsea in 1983 when the club was toiling in the Second

Division. He notched two goals on his debut and finished the season with 28 league goals to win the Golden Boot. Chelsea won the league and earned promotion back to the top flight after being relegated in 1978-79. Dixon won another Golden Boot in 1984-85 with 24 markers, but Chelsea was relegated again after the 1987-88 campaign. Dixon then posted 25 league goals to help them win the Second Division in 1988-89. He netted 193 goals in 420 contests before leaving for Southampton in 1992.

4. Didier Drogba enjoyed two stints at Chelsea with 164 goals in 381 appearances. The Ivory Coast international joined the side in 2004 from Marseille and stayed until 2012 when he headed to China. Chelsea then reacquired him from the Turkish team Galatasaray in 2014 because he wanted to play for manager José Mourinho again. Drogba, who is currently Ivory Coast's all-time top scorer with 65 goals in 105 outings, left for the Montreal Impact in 2015 after winning 14 team trophies, two Golden Boots, and several other individual honors with Chelsea.

5. Between 1948 and 1956, Roy Bentley scored 150 times in 367 matches for the Blues after the English international forward joined from Newcastle United and before leaving for Fulham. Bentley captained the side to its first league title in 1954-55 when they won the First Division. He also became the first player from Chelsea to play for England at a FIFA World Cup tournament when he was a member of the 1950 squad in Brazil.

6. Peter Osgood left his bricklaying job to try his hand at pro soccer, and he obviously made the right choice. The youngster was granted a trial at Chelsea after his uncle wrote to the club, and he joined the team in February 1964. He was just 17 years old when debuting in a League Cup match in which he scored both goals in a 2-0 triumph over Workington AFC. Osgood left for Southampton in 1974 but returned for the 1978-79 campaign, which was his last. He made 380 appearances and scored 150 goals, and he also helped the side win an FA Cup and European Cup Winners' Cup. A statue of Osgood stands outside of Stamford Bridge.

7. With two Golden Boots for Chelsea and 132 goals in just 169 games, striker Jimmy Greaves was arguably the club's most prolific scorer. He kicked off his pro career with the team from 1957 to 1961 before joining AC Milan. When retiring in 1980, Greaves had racked up 44 goals in 57 games for England and tallied over 400 times in approximately 600 games during his club career. He's also Tottenham Hotspur's highest-ever scorer with 266 goals, and his 357 markers is the most ever in the English top-flight. Greaves led the First Division in scoring six times but unfortunately didn't manage to win a team trophy with Chelsea.

8. George Mills chipped in with 125 goals in 229 appearances with the Blues, even though he wasn't always a regular starter. The forward was signed from Bromley in 1929 and netted 14 goals to help the side earn

promotion in his first season. Mills played just three times for England but was one of just a few players to notch a hat-trick in his national debut. He hung up his boots in 1943 and later worked as a coach with Chelsea.

9. Belgian international midfielder Eden Hazard joined the Blues in June 2012 from Lille in France and remained until leaving for Real Madrid in 2019. He was sold for a Chelsea-record £103.5 million after signing for a reported £32 million. Hazard notched 110 goals in 272 appearances and helped the squad capture the UEFA Europa League in his first campaign. He took home the PFA Young Player of the Year award in his second season. In 2014-15, he helped the team capture the League Cup and Premier League double and won the FWA Footballer of the Year and the PFA Players' Player of the Year awards. Hazard won six team and several individual awards with Chelsea.

10. The 10th all-time leading scorer for Chelsea is George Hilsdon, who joined from West Ham United in 1906 and was reportedly paid the princely sum of £4 a week. He scored five times in his debut and later tallied a team-record six goals in an FA Cup match against Worksop Town. Hilsdon netted 27 goals in his first Chelsea campaign to help them earn promotion to the First Division in their second season of operation. He was also the first Chelsea player to score 100 goals and finished his Blues career with 108 in 164 games before returning to West Ham in 1912.

CONCLUSION

After two 50-year droughts without a major league title to their name, some fans may have given up. But not Chelsea supporters. They've always stood by their team since it was formed in 1905 and always will.

The intriguing Chelsea story continues to be written and recorded because the club has now become one of the strongest and most consistent in the world.

With numerous pieces of silverware won by the squad in recent years, the club and its fans alike are determined to add even more to the trophy room as soon as possible.

The trivia and fact book you've just read details the club's history from the day it was born right up to February 2021 in another infamous, Covid-19-related campaign. We've provided a wide assortment of facts and figures concerning the Blues in a fun quiz style along with anecdotes and "Did You Know?" facts.

These include information on the most famous players and managers as well as controversial moments, transfers, and ups and downs. We've tried to include as many characters as possible, but with the club's history being so long and varied, we apologize if your favorites have gone missing in action.

Still, you'll have ample opportunity to relive the highs and lows of this storied club and adequately prepare yourself for the next Chelsea trivia challenge that comes your way.

Chelsea supporters have proven over the years to be among the most passionate, vocal, and knowledgeable across the globe, and now you'll have the perfect chance to prove it.

Thanks again for standing by the team regardless of the outcome and taking the time to read through our newest Chelsea FC trivia and fact book.

Made in the USA
Coppell, TX
10 February 2023

12441665R00075